WE ARE ALL ALIKE...
WE ARE ALL DIFFERENT

written and illustrated by
the Cheltenham Elementary School Kindergartners

Photographs by Laura Dwight

SCHOLASTIC INC.
NEW YORK TORONTO LONDON AUCKLAND SYDNEY

This book is dedicated to children everywhere.

"We are all alike ...
We all have hearts and brains.

We are all different ...
We do not think or feel the same way."

— the Kindergartners at Cheltenham Elementary School

Library of Congress Cataloging-in-Publication Data

We are all alike — we are all different/written and illustrated by the Cheltenham
Elementary School Kindergartners; photographs by Laura Dwight.
p. cm.

Summary: Kindergarten children describe the likenesses and differences among themselves.

ISBN 0-590-49173-3

1. School children — Juvenile literature. 2. Intercultural education
— Juvenile literature. [1. Individuality. 2. Children's writings.
3. Children's art.] 3. Cheltenham Elementary School (Cheltenham, Pa.)

LC208.W4 1991
370.19'6 — dc20   91-34264
CIP   AC

Designed by Leslie Bauman

Photographs © 1991 Laura Dwight

Copyright © 1991 by Scholastic Inc.

All rights reserved. Published by Scholastic Inc.

12 11 10 9 8 7 6 5 4   2 3 4 5 6/9
Printed in the U.S.A.   0/8

Special thanks to Jolene Byer, Lillian Colon, Marion Greenwood, Bill Gordh, Symirna Jean-Simon,
Derick Melander, Marcia Orellano, Deborah Owens, Nancy Phillips, Suzanne Richards, Magda Santos,
Bill Sparks, Monique Tabbs, and Karen Taliaferro.

About This Book ...

Welcome to this lovely book written by young children for young children. Based on the faith that young children could author and illustrate a book that would help young children enjoy learning about diversity, the Scholastic Early Childhood Division, with Cabbage Patch Kids® as a sponsor, created an awards program that invited preschool and kindergarten children and their teachers from around the country to submit original class-made books for publication. *We Are All Alike ... We Are All Different*, one of the winning books, is a greatly needed resource for parents of young children and early childhood teachers.

Understanding how we are alike and different is essential to children's development of the intellectual and emotional abilities necessary for living happily and justly with the wide range of human diversity in our society and world. By creating this book, "with a little help" from their teacher, the kindergarten children at the Cheltenham Elementary School had a rich and developmentally appropriate opportunity to explore the many similarities and differences among themselves. By doing so, they grew in self-esteem and comfortable, empathetic awareness of each other. Each child had the chance to recognize the basic human connections in us all: "We all have a body." "We all play."

Read *We Are All Alike ... We Are All Different* to the children in your program or at home to initiate awareness and exploration of similarities and differences. Each page can be a starting point for discussion that can enrich language development as well as children's understanding of diversity. The discussions sparked by *We Are All Alike ... We Are All Different* can form the basis for creating language experience charts and books among your children. Most of all, enjoy the wonderful adventure of learning about how we are all alike and different at the same time.

— Louise Derman Sparks

Louise Derman Sparks — a final judge in the Cabbage Patch Kids/Scholastic "We Are Different ... We Are Alike" Creative Teacher Awards Program — *has worked for 25 years with the many-faceted issues of diversity and social justice as a teacher of children and adults, child-care center director, researcher, parent, activist, and author. She is currently a faculty member of Pacific Oaks College and is the author of* Anti-Bias Curriculum: Tools for Empowering Young Children.

We are all alike.
We are all people.

We are all different.
We do not look the same.

We have different color eyes.
We have different color hair.
Some of us have curly hair.
Some of us have straight hair.
Some of us wear glasses.

We have different color skin.
Some of us have darker skin.
Some of us have lighter skin.

What color are your hair,
your skin, your eyes?

We are all alike.
We all have bodies.

We are all different.

Some of us are girls.
Some of us are boys.

Some of us are big.
Some of us are little.

What does your body look like?

We are all alike.
We all have families.

We are all different.
Some of us live with moms.
Some of us live with dads.
Some of us live with moms and dads.

Some of us live with grandmoms
and grandads.
Some of us live with brothers
and sisters.

Some of us look like our moms and dads.
Some of us look different from our
moms and dads.

What is your family like?

We are all alike.
We all live somewhere.

We are all different.

Some of us live in the city.
Some of us live in the country.
Some of us live in apartments.
Some of us live in houses.
Some of us live in trailers.

Where do you live?

We are all alike.
We all eat.

We are all different.
We like different foods.

What do you like to eat?
What don't you like to eat?

We are all alike.
We all like to play.

We are all different.

Some of us like to pretend.
Some of us like to climb.
Some of us like to read.
Some of us like to play ball.

What do you like to do?

We are all alike.
We are all different.

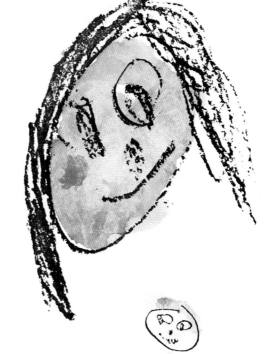

We are a family.

Meet the Authors and Illustrators: **The 1991 Kindergarten Class at Cheltenham Elementary School** *(Pictured above from left to right)*: **fourth row:** Rosalind Goldberg, teacher; Michael Di Stefano; Jesse Morgan Cohen; Andrew Meehan; Lauren Hirsh; Tiffany Spady; Noam Zerubavel; Dara Yoon; Kathy Roux, teacher's aide; **third row:** Robert Moffitt; Nathalie Montilla; Jon Park; Yaniz Estrada; Joseph Widmeier; Bridgit Clark; Thomas McCracken; Rell Williams; **second row:** Julie Eisen; Carlie Sweeney; Bari Goldberg; Matt Fischer; Stephen King; Palmer Aikens; Karla Brown; **first row:** Michael Hunter; Sean McGee. **Not pictured:** Colleen Walsh

Note: *The children featured above are not those featured throughout the book. The photographs of children appearing throughout the book were taken by Laura Dwight.*

About The Program: *We Are Different ... We Are Alike*

The Cabbage Patch Kids®/Scholastic Creative Teacher Awards Program, "We Are Different ... We Are Alike," was created to promote multicultural values and the acceptance of others. Children and teachers from preschools, child-care centers, and public and private kindergartens all over the United States (U.S. territories and Canada) submitted over 200 class-made books based on this universal theme. After carefully reviewing each entry, We Are All Alike ... We Are All Different *was selected as a winning book to be published by Scholastic. Following is an account of how this special book was conceived and written by the kindergarten children at Cheltenham Elementary School in Cheltenham, Pennsylvania, by their teacher, Rosalind Goldberg.*

No book is written in a vacuum. Kindergarten authors, as do all authors, use their experience, imagination, and interests to create. At the heart of this book is the philosophy of a school, Cheltenham Elementary, that treats each child with respect for individual differences and individual uniqueness. Our school's philosophy encourages working as a team — a family, if you will — to encourage group goals.

The process by which this book was written began with a typical kindergarten curriculum — "Me and Differences." When I read about the Cabbage Patch/Scholastic Creative Teacher Awards Program, *We Are Different ... We Are Alike*, I decided to have my class enter. Our whole-language approach to reading encourages writing as an integral part of the process of learning to read and my class regularly wrote and "published" books.

To create this book, we began with a science concept, "Snowflakes," which fit perfectly into likenesses and differences. From there, we brainstormed how children are like snowflakes — alike and different. After we discussed these concepts, I offered the children the opportunity to write a book and enter the awards program. They were very excited. We discussed the kinds of books that were their favorites. These turned out to be books that were predictable and repetitive. After taking down all of the children's ideas and words, I arranged them in the order that best reflected what they had described. Then the children drew their homes, their families, themselves, and other illustrations for the book. The individual pictures were copied, arranged in a collage, and painted by the children. By this time, although the children recognized their individual contributions, we realized how much we had worked *together* to create the finished product. This, in fact, was the goal of the project, that each of us is a discreet and unique whole, and the total group depends on participation by everyone.

Rosalind Goldberg
Kindergarten Teacher
Cheltenham Elementary School